It's your 1

Just
L.E.A.P.

*Messages that
will inspire you
to embrace life*

EVA M. KENNEDY

outskirts
press

Just
L.E.A.P.

Live life for you.
Expect good things to happen.
Accept the things you can't change.
Prosper in all areas of life.

DEDICATION

To my mom, Georgia Mae Kennedy. She sacrificed much and I stand on her shoulders. It is her courage and strength that dares me to dream and pursue the life I desire. She will always be the love of my life.

ACKNOWLEDGEMENTS

I have met some amazing, courageous, strong, and talented women. Although some were only for a season, I realize that every encounter was for a reason. Some have become close friends, mentors, and acquaintances. I am grateful for each one of them.

I am thankful and blessed for the love and support of my oldest and dearest friends, Bobbie Bell, Janice Taylor, Ubong Ituen, and Christine Sullivan. I wouldn't be where I am today without them. They have been my sounding board, never doubted me, helped boast my confidence when I didn't believe in myself, and held a space that encouraged me to keep pursuing my dreams. It is because of their unwavering love and commitment that I am able to be my authentic self.

I want to thank my family for always believing in me. Their love and support mean everything to me.

A special shout out and thanks to all of the women in the U HAVE THE POWER Facebook Group. I am grateful for this platform and appreciate you for joining me on Sunday mornings. You are amazing!

Table of Contents

INTRODUCTION

More often than not, so many women find themselves suppressing what they desire most in life. They bury their desires and live a life that is acceptable, but not necessarily fulfilling or rewarding. However, they will not hesitate to support and help others fulfill their dreams.

As I am writing, I am reminded of my mom. She left her husband and moved from a small town in South Carolina to Boston, Massachusetts, with four children and a tenth-grade education. My mom dedicated her life to taking care of her children. We were her priority; she sacrificed everything and lived for us.

One of my biggest regrets is that I never knew or asked my mom what she was passionate about, or if she had dreams of her own. This is one of the reasons I am passionate, dedicated, and committed to providing encouragement and support to empower women to live the life they desire.

In 2017 I created the U HAVE THE POWER Facebook Group. I use this platform to provide weekly inspiring and thought-provoking messages to support, encourage, and empower women to live the life they want.

It all started when my friend and life coach, Megan Farry, suggested that I go live in the group on Sunday mornings. She said that my message would resonate with the women in the group. After running out of excuses as to why I shouldn't go live in the group, finally I did it. I started Coffee Talk.

Now every Sunday morning at 7:30 a.m., I am live in the group doing Coffee Talk, providing a powerful and inspiring message. *Inspirations for the Soul* is the first book I authored, which includes some of the messages shared in the group. *Just L.E.A.P.* is a continuation; however, the messages have evolved over time.

My hope is that *Just L.E.A.P.* will be a good resource to help put the attention on you, so you can focus and pursue your dreams.

To hear an inspiring and powerful message weekly, join my Facebook Group, U HAVE THE POWER. https://www.facebook.com/groups/uhavethepower

Be confident. Just L.E.A.P. into your own!

LIVE LIFE FOR YOU

In too many instances, because of a woman's desire and commitment to help others she fails to think of herself as worthy to pursue her own dreams. She believes that when the needs of others who are depending on her are met, only then she can think about pursuing her own desires. However, she fails to realize that may never happen. There will always be others or some need that will require her help.

Live life for you is about learning how to focus on you. I don't mean from a narcissistic, ego, "it's all about me" perspective, but by being authentic and pursing your passion. I'm talking about pursuing the thing that brings joy to your soul, and using your skills, talents and experiences to make a difference in others' lives.

You may be thinking you've been helping others all of your life. Although this may be true, you may be helping others and doing what they need you to do. This is about declaring that it's your time to pursue your passion verses you helping others pursue theirs. It's time for you to make decisions based on what's right for you verses others making decisions for you, based on what's best for them.

It's is your time to make a commitment to yourself and live life for you. To be intentional, plan for growth, and pursue your passion. When you connect with your passion, and use it to find and understand your purpose, you will step into your own. This will bring you joy and put you on the path to living a life that is purposeful and more fulfilling for you.

YOU HAVE IT ALL

Remember when your parents told you to do something and you didn't do it? Or you did just the opposite of what they told you to do? As a child, even though they didn't give you a choice, you did it your way. You disobeyed them, and in some instances you were punished for it. You never thought about the fact that parents know what's best for their children. They want to keep their children safe and protect them from harm.

Even as an adult, your parents or an elder may have given you some good advice that you didn't listen to. Although you heard what they said, you did it your way. You didn't consider that they loved you. They had wisdom, experience, clarity and wanted what was best for you.

Today, you have that same protection, wisdom, clarity, and experience available to you. Within each of us lies a vast array of resources—everything we need to manifest the fullest expression of our purpose and our destiny. It's your inner being. This is your source, the leader within you. The key attributes of your inner being are wisdom, compassion, courage, clarity, and certainty. It has access to all the wisdom that ever was, has been there and back, and knows that ultimately everything turns out just fine.

Your inner being loves you completely and believes in you without question. It is grounded and can see quickly what is needed and how best to move forward. Your inner being has always been part of you and is eager to be more available to you. It is fearless and relentless in pursuit of the very best for you. Be still, meditate, and spend time connecting to your inner being.

Although you don't know what's up ahead, trust, listen, obey, and be guided by your inner being. It will give you what you need and take you where you need to go.

IT IS WITHIN YOU.

_____
_____
_____
_____
_____
_____
_____
_____
_____
_____
_____
_____
_____
_____
_____
_____

YOUR FUTURE
BELONGS TO YOU

You are one of a kind, with gifts and purpose, here for a reason. Dreams and desires that are unique to you have been placed on your heart, and only you can fulfill them. If you think back to your childhood, you can probably remember when you first discovered an interest or talent or even certain experiences or encounters that you now know were forming you. If you think long and hard enough, you can probably still remember the excitement you experienced, but now you have lost interest.

Sometimes life can be so challenging and painful that we lose interest in what was once exciting to us. As a result, we don't pursue what's been placed on our heart. We shut down emotionally and disengage with the person within, believing that life is hard and it won't get better. If you can relate and find that you have shut down and are not ready to deal with your emotions and move forward, then you won't be able to so.

It's important to remember that whatever we believe to be true is what's going to show up in our lives. If we believe something is too hard, then it will be too hard, and we won't be able to do it. However, be aware of what you are afraid of resisting and defending, and why. Dig deep to tap into your emotions and acknowledge them. Feeling pain and emotions is essential to finding out what needs healing in your life. Be with your emotions so you can understand what is causing them.

Start by engaging with your inner being, which can lead to real intimacy. Identify what negativity you have told yourself or allowed to take root in your life. Be conscious of how and what you are feeling. Are you feeling fear, shame, hurt, anger, or sadness? Whatever you are experiencing, ask yourself why and be truthful. Ask why again, and again. The more you are able to work through your emotions, the fuller your life will be. Eventually you'll find the truth, what you unknowingly believe that needs to be addressed, and work through it.

YOU ARE FREE TO MOVE AROUND.

THE LEADER IN YOU

I read that there is a difference between *living* your life verses *leading* it. Someone who is living their life does not plan and gives little thought about what they do with their day. They don't consider life as a gift and miss out on making each day count. They avoid responsibility, and daydream about tomorrow, imaging some better situation when life will be good. To avoid being accountable, they don't rely on themselves, but take direction from others. They go along willing to accept whatever life or someone else throws at them. As a result, they live someone else's plan.

Conversely, people who are leading their lives take ownership of their days and plan for growth. They live and understand that everything is done for a greater purpose.

If you are ready to take ownership and make a commitment to *leading* your life instead of just *living* it, then pursue your purpose. You were created for a purpose and designed to use your innate skills and talents to bless others. If light represents going forward and leading your life and darkness represents remaining in the space of living your life—not being accountable—then go for the light.

Embrace leading your life and let your light shine. This will bring joy to your soul. When people see your light shining, they will want what you have and it will provide an opportunity for you to share with others your purpose. This is important because life without purpose can be meaningless.

YOU HAVE PURPOSE.

IT'S TIME TO BE SEEN

Vulnerability weaves its way into our self-worth by reminding us of all the times we put ourselves out there and didn't measure up. It makes us remember moments when we've shared the depths of our heart and were met with ridicule or judgment. Vulnerability can suck the life out of us and makes a strong case for fake living.

Vulnerability is real; it's powerful, and has stolen so much. The thought of being vulnerable can prevent us from being authentic because it says who we are is not OK. Deep down inside, we believe that who we are is unacceptable, not good enough, so we present another version, one that looks less emotional and more put together.

We should not hide from vulnerability. We were not meant to live tucked away, hiding in our feelings of *"I'm not good enough"* or *"I don't want to appear vulnerable."* However, it takes real commitment to be honest about who we are and what we think, and real guts to stand up and speak out for what we want in life. It takes love, understanding, and grace to navigate it all. Once we address the feeling of being vulnerable, we are free to be real.

We matter and when we live from a place of authenticity it tells the world that we have embraced who we are—flaws and all.

PRESENT THE REAL YOU.

BE AWARE

How many times has a particular person you know knocked at your door and you haven't opened it? You tiptoed to the door, looked through the peephole, and decided you didn't want to be bothered so you didn't open it. Or you let them in but regretted it immediately, and it seemed like they stayed forever.

There may be various reasons why you didn't let this person in. Maybe it's because they are negative, loud, rude, tell lies, and cause you to have anxiety. They constantly remind you that you can't be successful, you are not good enough. They put you down and cause you to doubt yourself. You feel like they are on a mission, deliberately trying to take away your confidence so that you will have low self-esteem and live a life of status quo.

Let me introduce you to the saboteur, your inner critic. It's the negative self-talk that's in your voice and lives in your head. Once you decide to make changes in your life, it will come calling and knocking at your door, forcing its way in. The saboteur is designed to stop you from making positive changes. Its purpose is to take away your confidence so you will continue to live a life of status quo.

The saboteur generates all your negative emotions, including stress, anxiety, self-doubt, anger, avoidance, procrastination, insensitivity, or discontent. Know that it is real. However, you can learn to recognize the saboteur, and choose not to entertain it. Don't be a victim to your emotions and allow the negative self-talk to keep you from living your life. Intercept and discredit the saboteur with positive thoughts. No matter how many times the saboteur shows up or the number of ways it's disguised, dismiss it. The more you discredit the saboteur the stronger you become.

THERE ARE ENDLESS POSSIBILITIES FOR YOU.

GET OUT THE WAY

Consider this. You made a decision to step outside your comfort zone and embark on a road trip to pursue what you desire. At the beginning you were feeling excited, like you could accomplish anything, with lots of enthusiasm, positive energy, confidence and ready to go. As time passes, you start to feel weary, less confident, with low energy and enthusiasm.

Although you continue on your road trip, you begin questioning, "Am I ever going to get there?" Up ahead you see an obstacle in the middle of the road and it's not moving. You hit the brakes and proceed slowly. Eventually you come to a complete stop.

Now you have to decide if you want to go around the obstacle, so you sit and ponder. After a few minutes, you start to get frustrated, feel anxious, and realize your heart rate is up, beating faster than normal. You began to question yourself, "What shall I do? Shall I try to go around it? Do I just sit still? Or do I turn around and go back?"

You may be unknowingly causing the obstacle in the road. Although it took effort to step outside your comfort zone into the unknown and embark on this journey to pursue your desires, you are afraid to continue. Fear and lack of patience, commitment, skills, knowledge, or experiences may cause you to have anxiety and start to question yourself.

You are tired of staying focused and not seeing the results you would like. You want things to change now, so you begin to lose the enthusiasm you once had. You have been down this road before, didn't succeed, and now you are questioning yourself, "Will I ever reach my destiny?"

Although going beyond your comfort zone can cause negative emotions, know that life will give you the skills, knowledge, and everything needed to achieve what you desire. You may feel this is your biggest obstacle yet, but be mindful: you've been in training for it. Everything you have endured and learned has prepared you for this journey.

Use your wisdom, knowledge, and strength to go past obstacles for the sake of evolving into the person you want to become. You got this—keep moving.

OBSTACLES DON'T LIVE HERE ANYMORE.

_____

_____

_____

_____

_____

_____

_____

_____

_____

_____

_____

FRIENDSHIP

Although there is no such thing as perfect, we all yearn for genuine friendship. Also, we want to be that genuine friend for the people we care about, have established trust and honesty with, and have put in the time to build the foundation of getting to know each other. We want strong, healthy, and lasting friendships. We want to love and be loved. We want to give and receive mutual respect and share similar interests, activities, characteristics, and support.

We all want genuine friends who we know and are known by at the deepest level. Friends who will be truthful, help us to grow, and keep us out of trouble. Friends who will have our back, let us know when we are wrong, and if they drop the ball are big enough to take accountability and correct their actions—and vice versa. It is a blessing and joy when we have friendships like this that allow us to be our authentic self.

Think about this: if you have friends you can't be or express yourself with, or if you are not growing together, it may not be a compatible match or genuine friendship. If you are struggling with friends that are not authentic, I'm praying that you will take the next step to put in the time and go deeper, and then the next, and the next, until you have people in your life with whom you have actual intimacy. It is worth it to do the work to have genuine friends. We all need someone we can trust; it is a blessing to have that type of friend or be that type of friend.

Choose friends who will enrich your life and challenge you to grow. These types of friends are worth any struggle it takes to discover and deepen the relationship. Recently coined by one of the members of Coffee Talk, "Girlfriends are great, but GROWTHFRIENDS are better!"

RISK MAKING YOUR RELATIONSHIPS REAL.

_____

_____

_____

_____

_____

_____

_____

_____

_____

_____

_____

_____

_____

_____

_____

_____

_____

VALIDATION

It's easy to rely on others to keep you feeling good about yourself and make you feel approved. This type of approval-seeking behavior is intended to get consent and respect from others. In most cases, though, what people generally respect is the very opposite. They respect people who are true to themselves.

Seeking validation can prevent you from knowing who you are as a powerful human being—especially if you are making decisions based on someone else's approval, or not taking action because of fear of being rejected or judged. If you continually rely on others for answers or to boost your confidence, you are feeding self-doubt and low self-worth. This can cause you to feel discouraged, insignificant, or small if you don't meet their expectations or they don't give their approval.

You can't become so dependent on others that you're trying to get your worth and value from them. It is nice to have the approval of others but the way to get it is to have self-approval and self-respect. Focus on approving yourself. Connect to your inner being. It's always with you and has been with you all along, even if you aren't listening. The more you spend time connecting to your inner being, the less you will be guided to seek approval or the answers from others. Seek approval and value from within.

OWN YOUR POWER.

SHOW THE WORLD
WHO YOU ARE

We often use labels and details to describe ourselves, such as name, age, education, occupation, what we've accomplished, who we know, who we are friends with, where we live—and the list goes on. When you listen to a person describing themselves and they go on and on, you may think they are exaggerating, feeding their ego. If you say someone is feeding their ego or has a big ego, then you are saying they are too full of themselves.

I read that those with excessive egos do not adequately balance their desires with action. Instead, they act on what is most self-serving, instantaneous, and beneficial, otherwise known as immediate gratification. Others generally use ego simply to mean one's sense of self-worth, whether exaggerated or not.

We derive much value in cultivating and defending this ego and consider it our identity. The ego is part of who we are. When used in the exaggerated sense, ego is almost the same thing as conceit. However, it is not being egotistical to know you're good at what you do. Egotistical is when you don't have the competence and experience to back up your confidence. That kind of ego is worth criticizing. It's equally detrimental to be great at your work but downplay your value.

It is said the purpose of ego is to cause great levels of unhappiness and suffering so that hopefully one day, after trying to change the world and people around us, we can look inside and decide to change ourself. When we learn to recognize, manage, or check the ego, our own true, higher self will be experienced and demonstrated in the world.

DON'T LOSE SIGHT OF YOU.

LOOK FORWARD

Your thoughts can easily take control of your life and steer you in a direction you don't want to go. They dictate your actions, which can create your destiny, either good or bad. I encourage you to be clear about what you want to see in your life. Know what you want to accomplish and then throw everything you have at it. Step out of your comfort zone and go past what is familiar.

Tune into your life as if you're following an invisible path. Be committed and stay on course until you achieve what it is you want for your life. Remove the walls, or figure out how to go around them. Don't be afraid of failure or rejection. Don't confuse important commitments for the unimportant ones. Commitments will cost you time, and you can't create more of that. People chasing their ambitions get really good at saying no in just the right way.

Don't worry about others or what they say or think. Throw validation out the window. You are important and have the ability to make an impact on this world, if even just one person. You and me, meeting like this, is not a coincidence. There is work for you to do.

Today you get to decide if you are going to place limits on yourself or live life knowing there are limitless possibilities for you.

THE RACE IS YOURS TO WIN.

Life is an amazing, incredible journey. It's a gift and a privilege to participate in the journey. Everything you experience is an opportunity to evolve and be thankful.

I want to encourage you to think about your life. What are you putting off intentionally that you should be doing right now? Once you have identified it, simply decide not to put it off any-more and put a plan together. What will you do?

_____

_____

_____

_____

_____

_____

_____

_____

_____

_____

_____

_____

_____

_____

_____

_____

EXPECT GOOD THINGS TO HAPPEN

Whatever you desire, get ready and prepare for it to be a part of your life. Although you may not know how you are going to achieve it, or can't see it, do the work, believe, and have faith. Learn to live with the attitude of expecting good things to happen regardless of your circumstances.

Your expectations hold so much more power than you think. The type of life you live and enjoy can hinge on the concept of expectation. What you expect and think has a tremendous impact on everything that follows. Outcomes tend to follow where your expectation leads. Your expectations can determine your destination.

If you think and talk about what you expect then that's what you will get. Expect a better life and start by thinking of what you want to achieve. Keep your mind aligned with what you desire as the outcome. This can prepare you to accomplish great things.

Never forget: you are designed to live a great life. Maintain an attitude of expecting good things to happen. Stay focused, even in the midst of storms. Don't focus on where you are today in life, but where you are going. Be aware there will be times in your life when your human ability will reach its limit—life happens. Be unwilling to let the negatives in your life affect your expectancy to have a positive outcome. Don't allow the difficulties of life to lower your expectations. Always expect the best for you.

PREPARATION IS REQUIRED

Too often, we measure our success by comparing ourselves to other people. We see other people stepping into seasons of growth, abundance, approval, prosperity, and blessings. We find ourselves questioning, "What about me?" Although things might not be going well right now, expect change.

You may have been living with an attitude of expectancy for years and are still no closer to your destination than when you first started. There's an obstacle, another mountain in front of you. You may have come so close to that which you are seeking, you could touch it, taste it, feel it, only to have it pulled away. Now you feel used, forgotten, resentful, discouraged, and foolish to believe you can have what you desire. Although you want to keep trying, you are at the point of giving up.

Disappointments are inevitable; discouragement is a choice. Don't allow life's challenges to steal your enthusiasm or confidence. It doesn't matter what you've experienced in the past or what you may be up against in the present; you have what it takes to make it through.

If you are reading this and it resonates with you, there is work for you to do. You can start by changing how you see yourself. It's impossible to expect good things to happen for you if you are at odds with how you feel and see yourself. Even though things might not be going well right now, expect change. Don't allow the difficulties of life to make you think you deserve anything less than the best.

CHANGE IS COMING.

_____

_____

_____

_____

_____

_____

_____

_____

_____

_____

_____

_____

_____

_____

_____

_____

_____

_____

_____

A WHISPER OF HOPE

If you are the type of person who is always planning to do something, or have great things you dreamed about accomplishing but keep putting them off, maybe today is the day you should do something about it.

Today is the greatest gift you can receive. You will not get a do-over. Once this day passes, you will not get it back. Tomorrow has not been promised to any of us, so if you are putting your plans and dreams off until tomorrow, you should do them now.

Whatever you want for your future, take an actionable step today, plant the seeds and start the work now. If you are afraid to do what you know you need to do, pray about it, ask for help, and then do it. If you can't see past what's happening in your life today, then have hope and faith. Hope and faith may be the most valuable intangibles you can embrace.

Remember the times when you couldn't see your way through situations, but you didn't give in or give up. It was hope and faith that brought you through. Keep your mind on them and they will never fail you. Know that facts and what you are able to see with your natural eyes do not tell the whole story. Just because you don't see something in reality today does not mean you won't get it, or that it will not happen tomorrow. It's what you are unable to see with your eyes that may pave the way for authentic renewal and put you on the path to achieve what you have been dreaming about accomplishing.

Remind yourself every day that hope and faith is the foundation of pursuing the life that was meant for you. Embrace a relationship with them. Wrap your mind around all that hope and faith declare and promise. Hold on to them—they will see you through.

THERE IS MORE THAN THE EYES CAN SEE.

_____

_____

_____

_____

_____

_____

_____

_____

_____

_____

_____

_____

_____

_____

_____

_____

_____

_____

MIND YOUR SUCCESS

My curiosity got the best of me so I googled the number of thoughts the average person has per day. Although the numbers vary by source, according to Discover Magazine and National Science Foundation (NSF) some estimates include between 12,000 and 60,000 thoughts per day. I choose the higher numbers from HuffPost, which are indicated below. The average person has 50,000 to 70,000 thoughts per day, which equates to 35 to 48 thoughts per minute

- Our thoughts are repeated daily
- Approximately 95 percent of our thoughts today are the same thoughts we had yesterday
- About 80 percent of those thoughts are negative ones
- Tens of thousands of negative thoughts cycle through our minds day after day after day, poisoning our attitudes and our outlooks, one by one
- Eighty percent of tens of thousands of little thoughts add up to a lot of negative thinking and self-talk

If the majority of your thoughts are negative, then what do you think your actions will be? If your thoughts are negative, your actions and feelings will be negative as well. Whatever you are dwelling on in your mind will play out in your life.

Learn to replace negative thoughts. After you notice negative thoughts, you have the power to reject them. When you reject negative thoughts over time, they lose their power over you.

Toss out any thoughts that makes you feel hopeless, worried, or afraid. Refuse to entertain them in your mind. Each time you have a negative thought, expose it and replace it with a thought that is truer.

If the majority of your thoughts are positive, then you will feel and be more positive. Stay true to yourself. Always remember, you are creative, talented, powerful, resourceful, and whole—and capable of achieving what you desire.

WHAT YOU THINK BECOMES WHO YOU ARE.

_____

_____

_____

_____

_____

_____

_____

_____

_____

_____

_____

_____

_____

_____

_____

INSTANT AWAKENING

We live in an instant gratification world where we have been taught there is no need to wait for anything and there is a high level of expectation. Now a days you can just order it, and you will have it quickly. Some people want instant gratification and they expect it immediately. Instant gratification and expectation can be enjoyed and applied to many areas of one's life. However, if you have expectations or want something different for your life, you must be willing to do the work and wait for it.

Expectation can prepare you for what you are expecting. Again, you must be willing to do the work and wait for it. For example, you are expecting your first child. You have nine months to prepare. During the nine months you educate yourself on how to be a good mother and do the necessary work. You change your behavior, your thoughts change, and you do what's necessary to take care of yourself and be healthy. You have high expectations of being a good mother and having a healthy child because you are preparing for it.

When you expect greatness, you will receive it. Expecting greatness is easy when it is going on all around you. But when the going gets tough, and the light at the end of the tunnel seems far off and is getting smaller and smaller, expecting greatness becomes much more difficult. Although it may be difficult at times, expect it. Take responsibility and do the work. Believe in yourself. It will change your attitude and behavior. You will be far more effective and have greater appreciation of your accomplishments. Above all reasons, obstacles, or your own senses, believe in a positive outcome.

KNOW THE IMPACT OF YOUR WORK.

_____

_____

_____

_____

_____

_____

_____

_____

_____

_____

_____

_____

_____

_____

_____

_____

_____

_____

_____

_____

RENEWAL

The year 2020 will go down in history because of COVID-19. The impact was felt globally. Some places shut down completely. Everyone had to make adjustments and adapt to a new norm. We lost jobs, loved ones, and had to stand in line for food. We were forced to stay at home and wearing a mask was mandatory. It will be the most challenging year that some of us will experience in our lifetime.

Although COVID-19 presented many challenges and hardships in our lives, it also provided the opportunity for many of us to pause and reflect. We used the time to look at how we were living life. We thought about our struggles, where we are in life, and our experiences and determined what's important. As a result, we have become more aware and focused, and our lives have changed forever.

If you had a similar experience and used this time to pause and reflect and want something different, now is the time to make it happen. You can begin by looking at the totality of your life. If you have been allowing yourself to get bogged down by spending time on small things and making them bigger than what they are, be real and ask some hard questions. What's really going on with you? Then think about what you can do differently. Use your experiences, accomplishments, skills, knowledge, determination, and strength to help you make changes. Don't lose sight of what you want and commit to moving in the direction to achieve it.

CHANGE CAN BE GOOD FOR THE SOUL.

_____

_____

_____

_____

_____

_____

_____

_____

_____

_____

_____

_____

_____

_____

_____

_____

_____

_____

_____

_____

_____

_____

_____

_____

_____

A DIFFERENT VIEW

One morning, while standing on my tenth-floor balcony, I noticed this bird in the sky. It was circling and appeared to be looking at me. Initially, I thought it was a drone because the bird had perfect form. I kept looking at the bird, and the bird kept looking at me and circling. It got me to thinking, what could the bird see from its view, and what would I see if I looked at my life from the bird's view?

Have you ever felt like you were in a maze and didn't know what direction to take? You thought to yourself that if you had a view from up above you would know not only how to get out of the maze but also what was up ahead. If you looked at life from a different point of view, maybe it would all make sense. You would know what direction to take, decisions to make, and be able to see how the setup of your life leads to the essence of who you are, the ultimate plan, and your destiny.

Conversely, you may be able to see that you are exactly where you should be in life. You are positioned in the right direction headed for your destination. You are on track and what you are seeking is right there in front of you.

Take a look at your life. Are you pushing and criticizing yourself, without realizing you are exactly where you should be? If so, now you can stop being hard on yourself. Embrace what you have accomplished and focus on what you have learned along the way. You are a step closer and further along in life than you think. Get excited about what's up ahead.

THE SKY IS THE LIMIT.

_____

_____

_____

_____

_____

_____

_____

_____

_____

_____

_____

_____

_____

_____

_____

_____

_____

_____

_____

_____

A POSITIVE FUTURE

Each year you will endure challenges. We all do, but as you move forward, focus on bringing positive energy with you. Everything we go through is preparation to take us to the next level. If you are coming off a challenging year, remember how you felt and acknowledge how dramatic the year has been. Look at all the challenges, good and bad, positives and negatives, and think about what you want to do differently.

This is an opportunity for you to change. You don't have to rock the boat so to speak because much change is going on around us. You could say now it's an invitation to change. People are pushing past their comfort zones. They are longing to live life and show up differently.

Although there is still room for much improvement, women are part of change. They are standing up, speaking out, pursuing different opportunities, letting their voices be heard, and holding prominent positions in this country and around the world.

If you want different results you have to do different things. Become an advocate for yourself. If you are a victim of bullying or abuse, now more than ever, speak up and seek help if you need it, whether it be mental, physical, financial, or emotional. Use your voice and be part of change. You get to decide, to make decisions and choices to contribute to your own life, the culture, community, and society. You get to decide if life happens for you or to you.

THE TIME IS NOW.

A WISE MIND

I read online that there are three states of mind that we are all in at varying times: wise mind, reasonable mind, and emotional mind. Wise mind is the ideal state of mind that we strive for from which to make our decisions. In wise mind, we are aware of our feelings. We decide how to act in a way to honor our feelings and goals. The other two states of mind combine to form the wise mind.

Just like the three states of mind, every single person will go through different stages of life at varying times. These stages begin in our teens and carry us to post retirement. As we pass from one stage to the next we make decisions, endure, learn, grow, and mature in the process. At each stage we tend to reassess what's important and prioritize.

Spend some time and get to know where you are on your journey. Focus on your stage of life and state of mind. If you are looking at your circumstances right now and you are not in the place or space you want to be, use your wise mind to make decisions. Be honest with yourself and take responsibility to work through any unresolved issues. This will help you gain courage, confidence, and become a better person for it. Remain committed to your true self and desires.

USE THE MIND THAT KNOWS.

JOY BELONGS TO YOU

Joy is an internal feeling. It is not situational, guided, or based on something positive happening in life. Joy is an attitude of the heart and spirit. Although it takes discipline, you can experience and live a life filled with joy in every aspect. You can start by believing things will get better, regardless of the circumstances.

Your attitude can be either an asset, or a liability. There is no in-between. You are the source and get to decide how you experience life. Although joy begins in the heart and spirit, some people would say, "When my life gets better, I will have more joy." The reality is, if you change your attitude then your life will get better. It all depends on how you see things. For instance, the attitude that you have toward work can determine your level of success. It could be that you don't like your job and it shows in your attitude at work. Maybe if you displayed an attitude of joy, you could get a better job. If you change your approach, perhaps your outcome will change.

Don't allow the world and what's happening around you to dictate how you feel. If you allow your situation to dictate how you feel you may never live a life filled with joy. Your emotions will be guided by your situation. Be guided by your inner being. It can teach you how to live a life of joy.

Decide that you want to live a life filled with joy and hold on to that feeling. Believe that you can live a life filled with joy. Begin each day with an attitude of joy, regardless of what's going on in your life. Eventually, you will start to see and react to life differently. When you do, celebrate your progress. The joy you reap will propel you forward.

LIVE WITH IT.

_____

_____

_____

_____

_____

_____

_____

_____

_____

_____

_____

_____

_____

_____

_____

_____

_____

_____

_____

_____

YOU HOLD THE KEY

When someone says "You have an attitude" typically what they mean is your attitude is negative. Attitude is usually one of those things that only gets brought up when it's an issue. The word "attitude" has a negative connotation, but it isn't necessarily negative. We just don't often bring it up unless it is a problem. In reality, you always have an attitude. Every second of every day, you have an attitude. Not only do you have an attitude, but you are the one who makes the choice on whether or not to change that attitude.

Your attitude is going to be either positive, negative, or neutral. Be mindful—your attitude may seem trivial at times. However, your attitude is something that is going to shift you in a specific direction, and that direction is where you're going to go. If you have a pessimistic outlook, and a negative attitude, then negativity is probably all you are going to attract. If you are expecting to succeed or expecting to fail, then you probably will.

The choice is yours. Your attitude is the only thing in life that you can control all of the time. Although you won't always be able to control your circumstances or change your situation, you can always make the final decision on how they will affect your attitude. Your attitude is a tool; use it to your advantage.

BELIEVE FOR BETTER THINGS.

Change the way you think and it changes everything. If you are struggling in life, don't let how you see yourself today dictate how you will live life tomorrow. Think of what you want and be willing to do something different or uncomfortable to achieve it. Believe for something good to happen in your life—expect it. Be intentional on purpose and manage your expectations.

What will you do to create and maintain a mindset of expectancy?

_____

_____

_____

_____

_____

_____

_____

_____

_____

_____

_____

_____

_____

_____

_____

_____

ACCEPT THE THINGS
YOU CAN'T CHANGE

You cannot do anything about what is behind you, but you can do a great deal about what lies ahead. If you have been making bad choices and you want your life to change for the better, this has to change. You will need to make one good choice after another and be just as consistent as you were when you made the choices that produced negative results.

No matter what kind of trouble or difficulty you find yourself in, you can still have a blessed life. Allow your true self to rise to the surface. Do not be afraid to be you. Don't let how you see yourself today stop who you have the potential to become. See the beauty that you possess. Think of all that's possible and the incredible potential that lies ahead of you. You have the potential and ability to affect and impact change not only in your life but others as well. Changed people change people.

It's important to remember the past is an education, not a destination. Don't let things that don't matter too much matter too much. You can gain confidence, make positive decisions and choices, and change a negative attitude toward yourself or others. Live forward and know that you can make a difference. Regardless of what is happening in your life, know that it is building character and patience and giving you the experience needed to move forward.

You can serve as a light that leads others who may also find the strength to make positive changes and become the person they are meant to be. Give yourself permission to simply do and be your best.

STAND IN YOUR TRUTH

It's easy to be your authentic self when things are going well. However, it can be difficult when everything about your life feels like it's falling apart. Life can present you with challenges and sometimes it may seem that its more than you can handle. You feel like you can't go on—this is it. You feel afraid, not knowing if you can bounce back from this situation.

You may have self-pity, feel like no one understands what you are going through, and have many questions beginning with "Why me?" You may experience feelings of loneliness, discouragement and low self-esteem. You may get to the point where your faith waivers and you are ready to give up on hope. When you get to this point and you've done all you can, be your authentic self. When you are tired of fighting, stand in your truth.

Life can be hard sometimes; the lessons are painful and they can stop you dead in your tracks. At other times, in the midst of it all, you can experience joy. All of it is life.

Although you may not be able to see or understand it, no matter what is happening you are being shaped and prepared for the next phase of your life. Know that it's all connected, someway, somehow.

This is the time to embrace who you are, accept who you are, every aspect of you and everything about you. Be your authentic self and have hope for the future. Trust yourself. You are resilient and capable of handling more than you give yourself credit for. Know that everything is working together for your good.

PREPARE FOR SUCCESS.

FREEDOM

There may come a time when you start believing negative things about yourself. This could be caused by things people have done to harm you. This can include words that have been spoken carelessly about you and caused you pain and negatively impacted your life to the extent you begin to believe what others did to harm you is your fault. Although deep down inside you want to believe it's not your fault, you blame yourself. In your mind, there is no other logical explanation. However, you are tired of the pain and negativity and want to be free.

Let the truth be told, let it set you free. Separate the truth from the lies that you've believed. The truth exposes any lie that has held you captive. You can't control what people do or say. How others treated you, their brokenness, their negative, hateful, words, none of it was your fault. It was theirs. As scary and as painful as it may seem, when the truth is out it sets you on a path of healing, setting you free as you go. How others view you does not determine your worth or who you are. You are not responsible for the way they think. Don't dim your light to please them.

Face your pain, uncover any destructive lies you've believed about yourself, and submit to the process of healing and growth. The more you face your pain, the freer and more mature you become. Speak them out, acknowledge them, and then replace that narrative with truth of the beauty of who you are, so that you may live wholeheartedly.

When you no longer have anything to hide, you no longer have anything to hide. You're no longer afraid of your pain, no longer hiding in the shadows. When you accept the truth, you will find that bits of your heart are freer and places that you thought were ruined are healing. When you live openly, you begin to live differently. You will be able to exhale and take your next breath of truth, which is the basis of your entire being. It really does matter that you seek truth over feelings.

STEP OUT OF THE SHADOW.

_____

_____

_____

_____

_____

_____

_____

_____

_____

_____

_____

_____

_____

_____

_____

_____

IT'S TIME TO RISE UP

A new start is possible and a fresh hope is available regardless of where you are in life or your past. If you are holding onto a dream and still desire to achieve it, this is the season of spiritual growth and renewal—a time to refocus.

Consider Joe Biden, who ran for president in 1988 and 2008. Imagine the pain, uncertainty, and disappointments he must have felt when he didn't succeed the two times he ran for office. Although he held the position of vice president for two terms, his desire was to become president of the United States and he didn't give up. They said he was too old, but he didn't allow that to stop him. They said he had his chance and blew it; again, he didn't allow that to stop him. Now that he is the president, everything he endured both times he was defeated all seem like a distant memory.

Think of your own situation: have you allowed what happened in the past to dictate your future? If you didn't succeed but still have that burning desire, now is the time to try again. Only you can fully understand what you're going through, but if you know there is more to your life, keep moving. Address any holds the past may have over you. Don't let your emotions, pride, or ego keep you from trying again. Push past fear, doubt, loss, and shame. Let this season be the beginning of who you are truly meant to be.

I once read, "Broken can be restored. Sorrow can turn into joy.

Empty can be filled. Worthless can be valued. Not good enough can be desired, shame can fade, and confidence can arise."

Don't let your past choices, defeats, upbringing, culture, or treatment prevent you from fulfilling the purpose you are called to live.

YOUR DREAMS SERVES PURPOSE.

_____

_____

_____

_____

_____

_____

_____

_____

_____

_____

_____

_____

_____

_____

_____

_____

_____

_____

YOU ARE A NATURAL

Consider the life of a caterpillar; it matures into a butterfly. A caterpillar matures into what is already true about it. Because the caterpillar is a butterfly in essence, it will only display the behavior and attributes of a butterfly. Think about this. If you know there is more for you to accomplish, pursue it and be confident you will mature into what is already true about you.

If you've stopped believing in yourself or made a wrong decision, get ready to make your comeback. Now I know there are those who might say it's not that simple—particularly if there are other people involved. Your wrong decision may have set off a chain of events that can't be reversed. Maybe there are a lot of lives, yours included, that have been affected, but you can't rewrite the past. You have to go on from here, forgetting those things that are behind you and reaching forward to those things that are ahead. What's done is done.

You're not defined by your past; you're prepared by it. You have matured as a result of your past. If the past hadn't happened, you wouldn't be prepared for the better life that is coming your way. You are destined to evolve into the person you are meant to be. You can't help it, therefore accept it. You are a natural.

BE TRUE TO YOU.

KNOW WHAT IS IMPORTANT

Value yourself and know that you are deserving and worthy. These are important factors to living and being your authentic self. It's equally important to appreciate who you are and your qualities and take care of your physical and mental growth and developmental needs. It's a choice and a commitment.

Knowing your values and making decisions and choices that are aligned with them will give you a sense of appreciation of who you are. Although it does not necessarily mean it will be easy, you will have the satisfaction and peace of knowing you are honoring your values and being your authentic self. This can have a healthy impact on your emotional well-being. When you go against your values, you can have the feeling of knowing you went against what's important to you and that can cause anxiety, stress, and tension.

You are in control of how you feel and the decisions and choices you make. Focus on the things you can change, those that can bring you peace, joy, love, and kindness. Although there may be things that weigh you down and cause anxiety, you can't blame others. Learn to appreciate yourself, life, and the universe, and be willing to give and help others along the way. Accept the things you can't change and learn to be the person you want to become.

YOU ARE THE KEEPER.

YOU ARE AMAZING—
LIVE LIKE IT

You may be feeling like you've been changing your whole life, slowly getting worse. That may be true in some areas, but you have been making progress in other areas. While you may not be all you want to be or where you want to be, you're not what or where you used to be. There are probably many things that have already changed. Let's start with the basics. If you are less negative, less selfish, or less anything, you've changed.

Sometimes you have to look at how far you have come to realize how much you changed and accomplished. It's so easy to think negatively about progress and growth—especially when you have high expectations and things don't pan out as expected. The greater the gap between expectation and reality, the greater the disappointment of perceived failure. This can prevent you from changing and discovering who you really are.

Don't dwell on the past and make excuses for not living and moving forward. Embrace and welcome change. Live future focused and be passionate about life; you are still here. Don't allow your past to make you miss out on future opportunities and experiences. Look forward to each day; grab on to it. Laugh and laugh often. Open up your mind, exchange old thoughts and behaviors for something new. Explore new interests.

Don't end each day being negative or regretful; be thankful. Connect to nature, feel it, see the beauty in all there is. Learn to react positively to every occurrence and seek the lesson to be learned. You are empowered to become all you are destined to be. Move forward with confidence and believe that your best days are still right in front of you.

CHANGE IS WELCOMED HERE.

_____

_____

_____

_____

_____

_____

_____

_____

_____

_____

_____

_____

_____

_____

_____

_____

_____

_____

_____

_____

JUST BE YOU

Be confident in who you are. If life has beat you down, get back up and take your life back. Stand in your truth and recognize the beauty of who you are. Use your experiences to bless others and serve as an inspiration that can help them live in freedom.

Share your true self with others and friends. Let them see and love the real you. Your friends may reject the real you, initially, when you show them the full person you are. You may need to have brave conversations with them and share mutual experiences that have shaped your life and how you relate to people. This conversation may include struggles you face, your deepest desires, fears about yourself, and dreams for the future. Some of this may seem to be scary stuff to talk about, yet to be open and live your life on this level is one of the greatest rewards.

Do not be afraid to be you. Know that you can create whatever life you desire. Believe it and take ownership for pursuing it. You are still standing and because of your experiences, you are stronger now than ever. Whatever you want is waiting for you.

EASE ON DOWN THE ROAD.

THE FIRST STEP

You get to decide who you want to be. You get to define who you are, so be the person you want to be. This is your decision, not your family, friends, or coworkers. They don't get to define you, not today. You must be clear that the person you are being is not for your family or friends. However, if this is the case, then you must decide what needs to happen in the future.

Know that the person you are being will impact what you believe, say, and do. Your values and beliefs are important; they inform your thoughts, words, and actions. The decisions you make are a reflection of them and they are always directed toward a specific purpose. They help you to grow, develop, and create the future you want to experience. Your values system must reflect and be aligned with the person you are being. Otherwise, your moral system could be at risk if you are not using this as a guide to make decisions and choices.

Now is a great time to look at your values and beliefs. Use this as an opportunity to determine if you need to make changes and decide if you are making decisions and choices based on what's important to you. Once you stop using your values and beliefs as a guide, you could be at risk and become who others want you to be. When you look at your life, make sure you are comfortable with what you see and your values and beliefs are aligned with the reality of who you are.

If there are inconsistencies, then work through them so you

will have less stress and anxiety and be an overall healthier being, feeling better about yourself. Maintain a positive mindset
and manage your thoughts. Keep in mind: your thoughts control more than you can possibly imagine. They are the defining
shaper of your life. Your actions are the results of your beliefs
and your beliefs are defined by who you are. Don't lose sight of
who you are and the desires of your heart.

THIS ONE IS FOR YOU.

_____

_____

_____

_____

_____

_____

_____

_____

_____

_____

_____

_____

_____

_____

_____

_____

INVEST IN YOU

If you are emotional, or experiencing negative feelings of anger, rejection, fear, or unforgiveness, be aware and know the impact it's having on your life. Search your heart; feel and face what is happening within. Take time to focus on what's going on within you.

No one will get through this life without feeling emotions, making mistakes, or being hurt by others and hurting others. If you have an area you are struggling in—and we all do—don't ignore it or pretend it's not there, hoping it just goes away. It can remove love from your heart and control your mind. It's time to confront it. Feeling pain and emotions and confronting what is causing them is necessary so that you can work through them. By not confronting your feelings you could be holding your inner being hostage.

You will never conquer what you don't confront—especially if you are filling your time with substitutes, such as shopping, alcohol, drugs, food, gambling, or social media. In your journey to freedom there are no substitutes. It's time to draw a line in the sand, so to speak, and step over it. Remove anything that stops you from living the fullness of your freedom. You can learn to live a life that is without fear, anxiety, or worry. Think of it as a matter of the heart, necessary for your freedom.

I invite you to take the time and invest in you. This will help you focus on what matters most. When you live from the fullness of your freedom, you will begin to transform your life and the culture around you.

LEAVE NO STONES UNTURNED.

_____

_____

_____

_____

_____

_____

_____

_____

_____

_____

_____

_____

_____

_____

_____

_____

_____

_____

_____

_____

THE POWER OF CHOICE

No matter how much we try, we cannot fully control our circumstances. We cannot prevent trials and tribulations or eliminate risk or difficulty. What we can do is adopt a different perspective about our experiences. We can always choose the viewpoint we hold about any circumstance in our lives. The things that happen to us provide the chance to make our choices. It is like being dealt a hand of cards. We can't control what we are given but we do get to decide how to play.

It is our perception that sustains us, not the handling of our circumstances. The decisions and choices we make today affect our tomorrow. The responsibility of choices we make and how we respond to life belongs to each of us on our own. Choosing is something we should do based on what matters to us, what we've experienced, our values, and the purpose we are living toward.

Although it seems so obvious, it is so necessary. In order to have the life we want, we must choose and know we have chosen. To know we have chosen is a conscious internal kind of action. It is having a level of aliveness and meaning so that the choice is resonant and timely. Although resonant choices might not always feel good, even when they are based on honoring values and are aligned with life purpose, sometimes they are quite difficult. However, conscious choice means our actions are meaningful no matter how difficult.

The key here is choice—to choose to say yes to living a more fulfilling and balanced life. We don't have to wait for circumstances to be presented before we choose. We can be intentional and proactive verses making choices out of habit or being reactive. Our choices, thoughts, and actions are binding forces of true transformation. They either make every other shift in our life possible or destroy our chances of experiencing a life we desire.

YOU KNOW WHAT TO DO.

You are one of a kind and you matter. For those reasons I say, you are important. Sometimes it's easy to lose sight of that. It's easy to feel anything but important or lose hope when the organization you work for sees you as just another employee, or your family and friends take you for granted. Know that whatever job you are performing is important, otherwise you wouldn't be there and your family and friends wouldn't rely on you. Yes, you are somebody important, with unique skills and talents. You matter. You can't change that, accept it.

How comfortable is it for you to realize and accept that you are important? If it's uncomfortable, understand why. What will you do to change your mindset?

_____

_____

_____

_____

_____

_____

_____

_____

_____

_____

_____

_____

_____

PROSPER IN ALL AREAS OF LIFE

You have everything within you to prosper and thrive. It all starts with an internal perspective and how you process life. It is a state of mind. You can mentally achieve prosperity before physically accomplishing it. If you are looking at prosperity from an external situational perspective, you may never know what if feels like to be prosperous. Think of prosperity as internal harmony that has spiritual, mental, emotional, physical, and financial aspects—not sacrificing one for the other.

Before you accomplish anything in the physical realm, you must first accomplish it in your mind. If you are not prosperous in all areas of your life, then change your mindset—beginning with you feeling prosperous internally. Start focusing on your mindset and watch how things will change in your life. That mindset drives your behavior and actions. If you feel prosperous internally, it doesn't matter what your situation is at any given time; you will feel prosperous. It is not situational but how you view and feel about life, and yourself in general.

Know that you can prosper in all areas of life, so live like it.

BE THE DIFFERENCE

It is not unusual for some people to pause and think about their lives. They question themselves, "Who am I?" and "Who am I being?" If you can relate to this and want to take a moment to pause and think, I suggest you write your answers out on paper and consider the following:

- Who are you?
- Who are you being?
- Is this the person you want to be?
- Are you living the life you want to live?

Look at your answers. If you are not the person you want to be or living the life you want, what are the consequences?

Only you know if you want to make changes or are comfortable with who you are. Know that if you are ready to make changes, this could be the beginning of a new journey.

You can start by focusing and connecting with your inner being. Define what matters, your innermost passion, and get to know what you need to do to make life better for you. Learn to let go of what may be holding you back.

Commit to the changes you need to make. You have purpose, and when you pursue what's important you will not only take hold of it, but what's meaningful takes hold of you. Embrace it.

REPRESENT WHO YOU ARE.

_____

_____

_____

_____

_____

_____

_____

_____

_____

_____

_____

_____

_____

_____

_____

_____

_____

_____

_____

_____

_____

_____

_____

_____

_____

_____

BETTER THAN NORMAL

When will things go back to normal? This is a question we ask when things stop feeling normal or when we're in a challenging season where the end date seems unattainable. If you've gone through a challenging season, do you want to return to normal or a life that is better than normal? If you focus on returning to a normal life that's what you are going to get.

There is an old saying: "Be careful what you ask for because you might just get it." If you have wished that things will get back to normal, be clear of what you are asking for. Make sure it's not because you usually know what to expect, and find comfort in it, even if it's not good or healthy for you. Comfort doesn't always equate to a life that is healthy or good, or that we are experiencing peace and joy.

When we live through a hard season, it provides the opportunity to do some self-reflection and define what's most important. We endure emotional trials and keep moving. We go past normal, recover, and become stronger. The strength we gain is even more valuable. It helps us have a greater appreciation for life, live in the present, and be more intentional.

So, as you endure a challenging season and look forward to when things will get back to normal, don't overlook what you've learned and how you've grown. When you think about it, is it getting back to normal, or better than normal? Better than normal is meant to bring change to your life for all your life.

MOVE PAST WHAT IS EXPECTED.

CLARITY

Set aside some time to think about what you want in the months and years to come. Be clear, especially if you want more out of life. If you do not have a vision or dreams, it's time to tap into the person within. Spend some quiet time with your inner being, focus and meditate until you can determine what it is you desire.

Get a clear vision and create a plan. When there is no clear vision, you can quickly wander astray. Work your plan and keep in mind that wherever you are in life, you are not being kept from achieving what you desire. You are living and growing into it. Believe good things are in store for you. By doing so, you will stay inspired. Let go of anything that is putting limitations on what you can accomplish. Although it can be challenging, don't give up or give in.

On a personal note, once I decided to pursue my vision I worked diligently, identifying and working through obstacles. I had to tap into my inner being to remove the limitations they had on my life. Letting go and working through obstacles can be painful and difficult. Not working through them and letting go is even worse. However, when you do, you will realize that your future is much better than your past.

NO MORE SELF-IMPOSED LIMITS.

_____

_____

_____

_____

_____

_____

_____

_____

_____

_____

_____

_____

_____

_____

_____

_____

_____

_____

_____

_____

_____

_____

_____

_____

_____

_____

_____

YOU ARE THE CENTER

The mind can be noisy and busy. This can cause you to have negative thoughts and lose focus, which can cause stress and anxiety. When this happens, you can always refer back to the old saying: "Just breathe. You will feel better." One of the easiest ways to reduce stress and anxiety is to focus your attention on your breathing. When you focus on your breathing, it helps you center yourself and quiet the mind. This forces your stressors or anxiety to take a back seat.

This focused approach allows you be present and connect to your inner being. Staying connected to your inner being can help you manage life and stress by being aware what is going on within and around you. If you are not consciously aware, the day can go by without having an appreciation for what the day has to offer. You can miss out on the opportunity to just be a participant in the day, acknowledging yourself and living life as a gift—stopping to smell the roses, so to speak. You can fail to recognize what you contribute, or your own creativity, skills, and talents.

So if you find yourself feeling stress or anxious, just breath and connect to your inner being. You will realize there is much to be appreciated. Remain hopeful about what is ahead. Learn to be present in each day. Do not be distracted by what is behind you. Focus on what is in front of you. Learn to be at peace with yourself.

BE ALL IN.

LIVE BY DESIGN NOT BY DEFALUT

Process is defined as a series of actions or steps taken in order to achieve a particular end. Life is a journey and a process can help you achieve whatever you desire. If you have a desired outcome, then you should have a plan, with actionable steps. If you have fallen off or given up on your plan, starting today connect to your vision and start in a new place if need be. It's important to note, you are not starting over—*because you are not.* You are starting in a new place with experiences. Maintain your purpose in spite of difficulty, obstacles, or discouragement.

Start where you are and ask for help if need be. One of the worst things you can do is try to do it all on your own. If you need a therapist, coach, or mentor, get one. Don't be ashamed or afraid to ask for help. Don't let your pride get in the way of your journey. Cling to your friends and family for encouragement, prayer, support, and guidance. Believe in yourself and the decisions you've made, even if you have to change direction.

Remember, it's easy to give up, so don't. Know what's working, not working, what you are doing, and why you are doing it. Give yourself permission to go through whatever you are going through, feel it, and don't mask your emotions. Learn how to prioritize, and set goals and actionable steps, both short and long term.

Your journey doesn't need to start in a full sprint, but don't become stagnant. Take small steps if need be. Work your plan and make changes if necessary. Be flexible. There is a very specific purpose and plan for your life. Be persistent and committed to following through.

THIS JOURNEY IS ON YOU.

FORK IN THE ROAD

One day while out jogging, I made the decision to stop along the path at the fork in the road. I thought about my life and used the fork in the road to do some self-reflection and reinforce my decisions. The path to the right leads to a dead end. I viewed this dead end as living a life of status quo. I chose to stay to the left because the path continues. It represents my commitment to continue pursuing my dreams.

The fork in the road was my checkpoint, an opportunity to take a look at my life. I wanted to make sure my heart was is in the right place, and be clear about what I am doing and why I am doing it. I thought about my plan, vision, and goals to make sure they are realistic and are aligned with what I want to achieve. It helped me refocus and commit to running the race to achieve what I desire.

Since then, I have been more consistent, intentional, and on purpose. I've gotten better at managing fear of failure, and choose to no longer doubt myself and what I can accomplish.

If you are at a fork in the road and you must choose, here are a few thoughts for consideration:

- Will you have genuine peace about this path?
- Is this path appropriate for who you are?
- Does this path align with the overall plan for your life?
- Will the decision to pursue this path honor your values?
- Do you have the confidence to pursue this path?

Think of this as a moment in your life to make a major choice.

TRUST WHO YOU ARE.

_____

_____

_____

_____

_____

_____

_____

_____

_____

_____

_____

_____

_____

_____

_____

_____

_____

_____

_____

_____

_____

KEEP AN OPEN HEART

What do I want for my life? If you're like most people, that simple question can be very difficult to answer. Although there are some people who know what they want out of life, they are not ready to pursue it. They have their reasons. Maybe it is not the right time because they are taking care of elderly parents, children, or grandchildren. However, they are feeling anxious because of that deep desire inside for more.

On the other hand, there are people who don't know what they want out of life. They have that underlying desire for more, a yearning coming from deep within their soul, but can't get their arms around what it is. They have a persistent longing, knowing there is more. They can feel it, but it's hard to name or describe what it is they want. If you can relate to this situation, know that you are not alone and all the answers are within you.

For various reasons, you may have buried your desires deep within. Maybe you tried using your gifts and talents to pursue what you desire, but other people were critical of it to the extent it upset the balance of your friendships and other relationships. Or maybe other people felt uncomfortable with you pursuing your desires, which in turn made you uncomfortable. It was too much and became burdensome. As a result, you changed course or just stop believing in yourself.

Although your dreams or whatever you want for your life may be buried, they're still alive, within you. That's a good thing.

Your inner being has the answers you're looking for. Now is the time to seek guidance and listen to it.

Perhaps you are questioning "What do I want for my life?" or "What's next for me?" Be authentic and genuine. If there was ever a time to push past your fear it's now. It's time to define and boldly represent who you are.

SHINE YOUR LIGHT.

_____

_____

_____

_____

_____

_____

_____

_____

_____

_____

_____

_____

_____

_____

_____

_____

RECOGNIZE IT

When you decide you want something or anything different in life, you have to do the work to achieve the desired outcome. Examples are an education, relationships, or starting a new job. With these examples there is a beginning and an outcome. There is the diploma, marriage, and a successful career. You know you have achieved what you pursued or desired when you reached or obtained that specific outcome.

What happens when you pursue what you desire, you pray for it, you wait on it, and it's right there but you don't recognize it? You want to be in a relationship and that person, your mate, is right in front of you and has been there all along. You are seeking a new job, but maybe you are in the perfect position for growth and opportunities and do not realize that this is the one.

The wait is over. Everything you've been waiting for is right in front of you. However, you are deliberately holding back, not seeing what is there to be seen. You are busy being defensive and afraid, and sabotaging yourself because of fear or feeling unworthy. You are thinking it's too good to be true, or you are not deserving of the job, home, relationship, etc.

Take a step and go for it. You are prepared. You are deserving, reliable, and trustworthy for others. It's time to trust yourself. See the goodness within yourself. You are intelligent, knowledgeable, dependable, supportive, and responsible. You wanted it, waited for it, now it's here. Be confident and enjoy it.

ASK AND YOU SHALL RECEIVE.

YOU CREATE YOUR
OWN REALITY

Be mindful of how you view the events, situations, and conditions in your life. When an event happens and you have negative feelings, you attract more conditions that represent your feelings. For example: you overslept for an appointment. Now you are running late and to make matters worse, you can't find your car keys. Immediately you began to feel negative emotions, and are angry and anxious. You've allowed this event to ruin your entire day.

Another approach to the same situation would be to remain neutral and allow it to play out. You overslept and there is nothing you can do about the moment in the moment. You could love the moment no matter what and look for positive aspects or you can be a victim. If you fight against the moment, it's a losing battle. You can't change what has already happened; it becomes the past. But you can change how you handle and approach it.

Every event, situation, and condition are there for you. There is something for you to discover about yourself in each and every condition. They are all there for you, to help you improve. Know that to expand and evolve you must constantly be changing. Although change can be uncomfortable, it can also be amazing. Changing your approach and thinking just a little can alter the course of your life dramatically. Transformation can happen in your life. If you change your thoughts, you will change how you exist.

Focus on the positives and learn to appreciate what is good about each moment. Whatever the experience is, lean into it joyously and view it as an opportunity to expand and grow. The experience you create represents who you are and who you want to be.

EVERYTHING IS POSSIBLE.

A WALK TO REMEMBER

One day while walking along the lakefront, I allowed my negative thoughts to get the best of me. I thought about what I didn't accomplish, what I could have done better, and failures verses successes. I began to feel anxious and disappointed. After a few minutes, I realized my mood had changed, as I was not in alignment with my inner being. I became intentional, changed my thoughts, and reminded myself of why I started this journey.

I started this journey because I was seeking my life's purpose. I was ready for more, but I didn't know how to move forward or what to do. I felt stuck and restless but knew there was more to my life. My past successes were insignificant. I had a yearning in my soul for something that I knew was bigger than me.

After much praying and asking God for guidance, I sat down and spent some time identifying, prioritizing, and defining my top five values. I knew from that point on, whatever I decided to do with my life had to be aligned with my values. Eventually I was led to coaching school. It was during this time I had my first emotional breakthrough. This was the beginning of an emotional journey.

I had to learn to acknowledge and confront my emotional issues. I grew up suppressing my feelings, doubting myself, believing I wasn't good enough and afraid to show any emotions. Although I didn't realize it, I had become an emotional prisoner, holding myself hostage. I didn't know how to be free. The skills, strategies, and techniques I learned in coaching school, along with hiring a coach, helped me tap into the person within. I had hungered to be free and now I was beginning to work through my emotions and felt a sense of freedom.

Eventually I was able to define my passion, which led me to my purpose. As far back as I can remember, I have always prayed, and I still do, asking God to use me to be a blessing to others. Finally, I knew who I wanted to help and how, which led me to my vision. I started my business, learned new skills, and developed tools and resources to support, encourage, and help women live the life they want.

Somehow in the mist of it all, I had allowed my focus and priorities to get twisted. I began to focus more on measuring the financial outcome verses helping women. I asked myself, "What is important?" This brought me back to the reality of what I am doing and why. I had to reconnect with my why, knowing that if I can have a positive impact on just one woman's life, I'm living my purpose. Therefore, I am successful. This is my passion; it brings me joy. I had to realize and acknowledge that success is not defined by my financials, but my ability to help and serve others.

I am grateful for the opportunity to do so. I have everything I prayed for and couldn't ask for greater success than that.

I reminded myself of what's important and made a list. I hope by sharing my list, it will help you.

- Live a life of purpose on purpose
- Stay connected to my why
- Stay connected and aligned with my inner being

- Live from a place of high-level positive energy
- Believe in myself
- Ask for help
- Make value-based decisions and choices
- Know the consequences of my choices
- Be present
- Be grateful
- Be more transparent
- Foster self-love, appreciation, and acceptance
- Respect and help others
- Live from a place of love verses fear
- Embrace and love life
- Hold onto hope and faith
- Be humble
- Trust God

SUCCESS IS WHAT YOU THINK IT IS.

Although change can be challenging, be willing to develop an attitude of prosperity. Don't be stubborn, become stagnant, and hunker down set in old ways. Make a commitment to continuous growth, create new habits, and do the work to evolve. Stay focused and don't waste time talking yourself out of pursuing what's important to you. Otherwise, living the life you desire may never be realized.

Give some thought to what you will do to create a mindset of prosperity? How will your attitude, behavior, and actions change?

_____

_____

_____

_____

_____

_____

_____

_____

_____

_____

_____

_____

_____

_____

_____

A Personal Note...

I am grateful to you for allowing me to be part of your journey. Although we have all experienced challenges and difficulties, through it all we are still here, part of the universe—yes, the universe, and all there is still exists and you and I are a part of it.

As you continue to grow, think about living from a place of consciousness and being mindful. If there is a restlessness in your heart, you feel there is something more for you to do, or if you are not being who you know you are supposed to be, then you must ask yourself, what do you want to do? Know that *it's up to you*, but consider the following:

- Do you want something different for your life?
- Do you have dreams?
- Do you want to evolve and grow?
- Do you want to be a better version of yourself?

If you answered yes to any of the questions, consider it time to raise the bar and start creating your life and being the person you want to be. Give your attention to what you want, not what you don't want. Be guided by your inner being.

Focus on being the highest version of YOU and just *be*:

- Be connected to your source
- Be committed to live an amazing life—your best life
- Be willing to go beyond your comfortable zone

- Be willing to look at life from a different perspective
- Be open and willing to grow and learn
- Be resilient—even through trials and tribulations
- Be courageous, in spite of fear
- Be in touch with your emotions—don't mask them
- Be vulnerable
- Be confident
- Be consistent
- Be grateful
- Be joyful
- Be hopeful
- Be kind to others and yourself
- Be positive
- Be humble
- Be thoughtful
- Be prayerful
- Be forgiving
- Be supportive
- Be able to recognize your strengths and weakness and know how to use them
- Be able to ask and receive help
- Be able to say "I don't know"
- Be able to prioritize and strategize
- Be able to say "NO"
- Be able to say "Yes"
- Be conscious and aware
- Be intentional
- Be the person you want to be
- Be the beauty of all you are
- Be yourself

Life is full of challenges, trials, and tribulations. Don't be afraid of them. Face them with faith, rather than reacting with fear, panic, and despair. Be courageous and focus on the positives. Instead of "What if I fail?" focus on "What if I succeed?" Be guided by all that is possible and know that you are the one to reach your destiny. Receive what it is you desire; the universe is ready to deliver it to you.

Live your life with love, joy, faith, and hope. Remember, you have experience!

Love + blessings,
Eva

"For I know the plans I have for you," declares
the Lord, *"plans to prosper you and not to harm
you, plans to give you hope and a future."*

Jeremiah 29:11

New International Version

About the Author

Eva M. Kennedy is the founder and principal of Eva M. Kennedy LLC /1Evalution, a boutique life coaching firm. She is a certified life coach, speaker, and author.

Eva is an accomplished leader with over twenty years of corporate experience. She achieved a key leadership position at Allstate Insurance Company. In her role as a director, Eva was responsible for designing, developing, and implementing countrywide operations and procedures with positive measurable impact on fifteen thousand employees. She is highly trained in matrix organization, leadership development, change management, organizational strategy, process design and implementation, and compliance.

After being diagnosed with breast cancer and a reoccurrence within five years, she took early retirement and left the corporate world in 2006. In the years following her retirement, Eva embarked upon a journey of self-discovery, which led her to coaching. Eva wanted to pursue her passion to help others, continue her own development, and find her purpose in life. She is excited and passionate about being a coach and helping others achieve personal and professional fulfillment. Her focus is on empowering women by helping them tap into the person within so they can live a purposeful and more fulfilling life.

Eva has authored and published two books, *Inspirations for the Soul* and a workbook, *Witness the Most Powerful YOU: Five Fundamental Principles to Create and Live the Life You Desire*. The workbook supports her workshop, "Witness the Most Powerful YOU." The principles are designed to help participants make decisions and choices by focusing on the person within. Eva is passionate about helping others choose to live the life they desire and enjoys facilitating her signature workshop.

Eva is an active volunteer and mentor. She believes in giving back and enjoys working with others to help them move forward.

CPSIA information can be obtained
at www.ICGtesting.com
Printed in the USA
LVHW040554280821
696211LV00001B/4